Transport Poems

Compiled by John Foster

OXFORD

Oxford University Press, Walton Street, Oxford, OX2 6DP

Oxford New York Toronto
Delhi Bombay Calcutta Madras Karachi
Kuala Lumpur Singapore Hong Kong Tokyo
Nairobi Dar es Salaam Cape Town
Melbourne Auckland Madrid

and associated companies in
Berlin Ibadan

Oxford is a trade mark of Oxford University Press

© Oxford University Press 1994
ISBN 0 19 916684 6
Printed in Hong Kong

CIP Catalogue record for this book is available from the British
Library

Acknowledgements
The Editor and Publisher wish to thank the following who have kindly
given their permission for the use of copyright material:

John Foster for 'The double-decker bus' and 'Driving along' both ©
1993 John Foster; Barbara Ireson for 'Two, one, zero' © 1975
Barbara Ireson, previously published in 'A bright, red lorry'
(Transworld); Tony Mitton for 'The Skateboard Twins', 'Many ways to
travel' and 'Mr Mad's machine' all © 1993 Tony Mitton; Brian Moses
for 'Waving at trains' © 1993 Brian Moses; Celia Warren for 'Night
ride' © 1993 Celia Warren.

Although every effort has been made to contact the owners of
copyright material, a few have been impossible to trace, but if they
contact the Publisher, correct acknowledgement will be made in
future editions.

Illustrations by
Jan Nesbit
Paul Dowling
Chris Smedley
Mark Vyvyan-Jones
Jenny Williams
Renée Andriani
Bucket

Many ways to travel

There are many ways to travel
and one that I like
is to zoom down a hill
on a mountain bike.

There are many ways to travel
and another that's nice
is to slide on a sledge
on the snow and ice.

There are many ways to travel
and isn't it fun
to sail on the sea
in the wind and sun?

There are many ways to travel
but the best by far
is to ride on a rocket
to a distant star.

Tony Mitton

The double-decker bus

We like riding
on the double-decker bus.
Up on the top-deck, that's the place for us.

In the front seat
with the driver down below,
We give the orders, tell him where to go.

We tell him when to speed up,
and when to slow down.
We drive the double-decker through the town.

4

We drive it up the hill
and park by the gate.
We make sure that the bus is never late.

We like riding
on the double-decker bus.
The front seat on the top deck—
That's the place for us!

John Foster

The Skateboard Twins

Here she comes,
Sally Green!
We all call her
the Skateboard Queen.

And here comes Sammy,
her best mate.
Sammy is a champ
on the kingsize-skate.

They swerve and they spin.
They never trip.
Sally does a twist
with a backward flip.

Sammy does a spinner
round the bins.
Sally and Sammy
are the Skateboard Twins!

Tony Mitton

Mr Mad's machine

Mr Mad has made a machine
To take you round the world.
Its wheels are square. Its tail is long.
Its wings are thin and curled.

It blows out rings of purple smoke.
The engine squeaks and squeals.
The jets are very powerful.
They're made of cotton reels.

I wonder what it would be like
To fly in the machine.
It is the strangest sort of plane
That I have ever seen!

Tony Mitton

Two, one, zero

Count down, count down,
Rocket leaving soon.
Count down, count down,
Leaving for the moon.

Count down, count down,
Minutes flicker by.
Count down, count down,
All eyes on the sky.

Count down to blast off,
Counting down from ten.
Count down to blast off,
For the rocket men.

Blast off! Blast off!
Rocket in the air.
I'd like to be an astronaut,
Alone in space up there.

Barbara Ireson

11

Driving along

Sometimes when I sit in my car,
In the driving seat,
I pretend that I am driving
Down a busy street.

I turn a corner carefully.
There are traffic lights ahead.
I put my foot down on the brake
Because they are turning red.

I steer past lots of other cars.
I overtake a bus.
I turn into a car park
And I find a place for us.

I go and buy the ticket.
I carefully lock the door.
Then, when Mum has done the shopping,
I drive her home once more.

John Foster

Night ride

When I can't sleep
I shut my door
And sit on the rug
On my bedroom floor.

I open the window.
I close my eyes
And say magic words
Till my carpet flies.

Zooming over gardens,
Chasing after bats,
Hooting like an owl
And frightening the cats.

Then when I feel sleepy
And dreams are in my head,
I fly back through my window
And snuggle down in bed.

Celia Warren

Waving at trains

I like to wave at trains
as they hurry down the track,
but when I stick my tongue out
nobody waves back.

Brian Moses

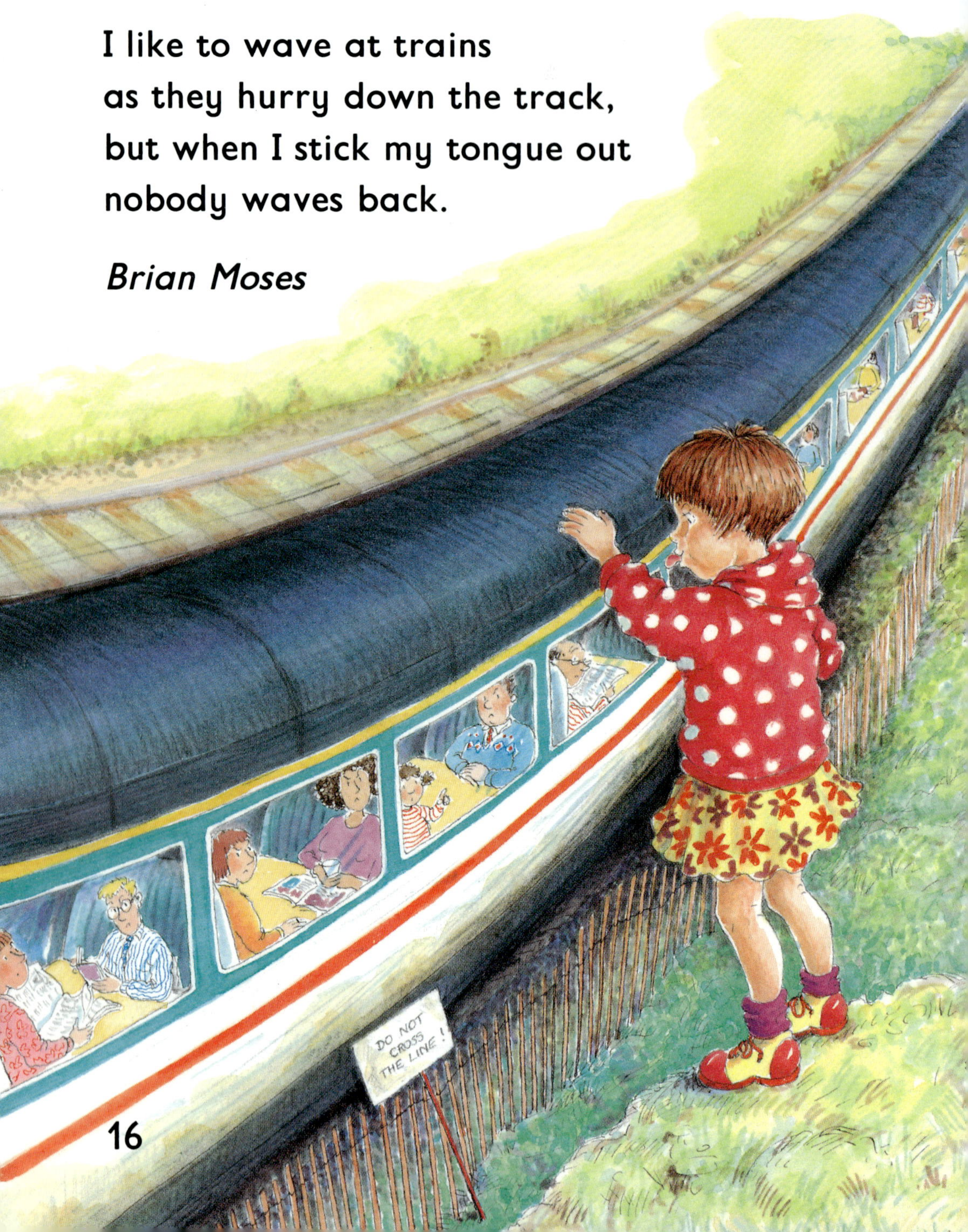